Original title:
The Absurdity of Life and Other Observations

Copyright © 2025 Creative Arts Management OÜ
All rights reserved.

Author: Julian Carmichael
ISBN HARDBACK: 978-1-80566-068-2
ISBN PAPERBACK: 978-1-80566-363-8

Dancing on the Precipice of Tomorrow

We twirl at the edge of quite a fall,
With shoes too tight and a silly call.
Tomorrow's fate is just a jest,
As we leap forward, we hope for the best.

Around us, the world spins askew,
A wobbly dance, and oh, how we pursue!
Laughter erupts from this crazy stage,
As we twinkle and whirl in life's grand page.

Echoes of a Laughing Universe

Stars giggle softly, casting bright light,
While we fumble in our silly plight.
A cosmic joke, we play our part,
Jesting as we trip on life's shopping cart.

Among planets twirling in a vast swirl,
We stand like children in a big, mad whirl.
With echoes of chuckles from up above,
We grin like fools, and that's our love.

Whispers in a Chaotic Symphony

In a world where nonsense holds the tune,
The moon winks at us, a playful boon.
With every note in this wild ballet,
We sway in rhythm, come what may.

Chaos whispers secrets, giggles in the breeze,
As we juggle our dreams with awkward ease.
Quirky melodies hug our delight,
And we dance through the fog of the night.

Jesters in the Court of Existence

Crowning ourselves with mismatched hats,
We skip through the halls where reason chitchats.
With jests and puns, we claim our crown,
In this royal farce, we won't back down.

The king throws pies, the queen sings flat,
While we prance about, like a cat with a spat.
In laughter and folly, we find our reign,
As jesters of life, we embrace the insane.

Searching for Sense in Chaotic Whirls

In a world where socks depart,
I'm left to ponder, where's the art?
The clock ticks loud, yet time stands still,
A dog in bowtie, chasing a quill.

Birds gossip about the weather,
While cats debate the meaning of tether.
A sandwich flies past in the breeze,
And I just sit, munching on cheese.

The Lament of Lost Logic

My goldfish wants to be a star,
He dreams of venues, near and far.
Yet here he swims in a bowl, confused,
While I ponder my dinner, slightly bruised.

The toaster talks to the old shoe,
While I make toast; it's all so askew.
A chair declares, 'I'm feeling quite grand',
As I trip over it, bread in hand.

Giggling Novels Left Unwritten

The pen wrote tales of wobbly bees,
Who danced with clocks in a light summer breeze.
Yet here I sit with a blank page bare,
Lost in a daydream, sipping stale air.

A plot unfolds where jellybeans sing,
While penguins wear hats—what a curious thing!
But logic escapes like a roguish thief,
Leaving me laughing on the brink of grief.

Sunsets Over the Silly Sea

The sun dips down, a rubber duck,
Bobbing gently, what a lucky luck!
Two crabs discuss the best way to dance,
While seaweed waves and takes a chance.

A seagull struts in a stylish hat,
Challenging waves like a chatty brat.
As stars poke through curtains of dusk,
I giggle at life, a cherished husk.

Questions Where Answers Should Be

Why do socks always go stray?
They vanish without a word to say.
Do pizzas dream of being round?
Such mysteries in the shapes we've found.

Why does the toaster burn the bread?
While coffee keeps us half awake instead.
Do chairs ponder their sitting fate?
Such questions arise while we await.

Shadows of Laughter in a Serious Gloom

The cat stares like it's seen the truth,
While I wonder if it remembers its youth.
Why do we pay for things so strange?
Like shampoo that promises to rearrange?

The sun peeks in, a cheeky grin,
While I'm busy losing my comfort zone spin.
A bird scoffs as it flits on by,
As if to say, 'Oh, give it a try!'

Unraveled Threads of Everyday Tapestry

The spaghetti's tangled like my thoughts,
Each twist and turn's what life begot.
Does cheese really have a golden age?
Or just a place on a food museum stage?

A frog croaks wisdom from a green bloom,
While I spiral deeper into my room.
Do dust bunnies plan a surprise escape?
Or scheme to give my allergies shape?

Surreal Conversations with a Blank Page

My pen dances, a chicken on the run,
Winging words in the blotting sun.
Does the ink know where it will go?
Or just wander where the wild thoughts flow?

The paper listens, a patient ear,
To absurd tales that draw quite near.
Will laughter echo in written form?
Or is it all just whimsical norm?

The Weight of a Feather in Strong Winds

A feather floats upon a breeze,
It flirts with life so light and free.
But add a gust, it turns and twirls,
Oh look, it dances, what a world!

A balloon deflates with a sigh,
While paper ships begin to cry.
Where do these whims of chance reside?
Perhaps in smiles that wind can hide.

A cat observes from lofty heights,
While on the ground, a dog takes flight.
Together they weave tales so grand,
In winds that whisk and swirl the sand.

A world of chaos at its best,
Where logic takes a little rest.
Just let it spin, this merry tale,
On wings of whimsy, we shall sail.

When Logic Takes a Backseat to Whimsy

A turtle wears a tiny hat,
While watching as the rabbit chats.
In tales absurd, they spend the day,
Oh logic, where did you stray?

A fish recites a poem loud,
To entertain a passing cloud.
With bubbles, laughter fills the air,
What curious thoughts swim everywhere!

A snail remarks, "I'll race today,"
While pigeons plot their grand ballet.
A world turned upside down, how nice,
To trade our woes for silly spice.

In winks and grins, we find our way,
Through maze of whims that twist and play.
For logic's lost, but never fear,
In playful hearts, the joy is clear.

Cactus Flowers Blooming in Concrete

A cactus grows where streets are bare,
Its blooms defy the stony glare.
In cracks of life, we find the cheer,
Of flowers brave that persevere.

The city hums with restless beats,
Yet blooms arise from stubborn feats.
Dandelions dance in the cracks,
Whispering secrets to the tracks.

Pigeons strut with deliberate grace,
While sunlight paints a warm embrace.
In urban jungles, green prevails,
Against the odds, true life exhales.

With laughter sprouting everywhere,
In paved places, blooms do dare.
So let the concrete wear its crown,
While nature laughs, and joy's renown.

Finding Clarity in a Cloudy Reflection

A mirror sits, all fogged and gleamed,
Reflecting dreams that once were deemed.
But who is that behind the glass?
A smiling ghost? A friendly pass?

Clouds of thought drift in a swirl,
As raindrops play their silly whirls.
I ponder life, yet find it vague,
As giggles hide beneath the fog.

A sunny day once filled with cheer,
Now twists to laughter mixed with fear.
Yet with each splash of silver rain,
I find a smile in the mundane.

So here in clouds, I shall reside,
Where clarity and whimsy collide.
And as reflections softly blend,
I'll dance in dreams until the end.

The Flimsy Walls We Build

We stack our bricks with care,
Yet every gust makes them sway.
Laughing at dreams, we dare,
As wisdom runs away.

With blueprints drawn in crayon,
Plans made on backs of old trays.
In the end, we carry on,
Building castles on sun rays.

Wobbly towers of tall tales,
Teetering on whims of fate.
Our logic fails but never pales,
What a lovely twist of fate!

Each crack is filled with laughter,
As we dance through life's delight.
Building walls that never matter,
What's enclosed is pure twilight.

Gazing at Clouds of Uncertainty

Drifting thoughts like cotton candy,
Swirling doubts in shades of gray.
Unspooled dreams that seem so dandy,
Caught between the night and day.

We chase shadows shaped like bunnies,
Under skies that swiftly change.
Laughter echoes, oh so funny,
In this world that's rather strange.

With every glance, the shapes do shift,
Unruly thoughts begin to bloom.
From confusion, joy we lift,
In this whimsically spun room.

Oh, the wonders we create,
As the clouds continue to fly.
Amidst it all, we celebrate,
With absurdities piled high!

Rhythms of a Raucous Reality

Life's a dance on slippery floors,
With partners who just won't stand still.
To each beat, our laughter roars,
We waltz on nonsense with thrill.

Our clocks tick backward, time's a joke,
Tickled dreams that never sleep.
With every stumble, we invoke,
Giggles buried in hearts so deep.

Each moment's a vibrant jest,
Chasing whims through fields of fun.
In this chaos, we're the best,
Making merry, on the run.

As the music plays its tune,
With silly steps, we share a glance.
In rhythms that burst like balloons,
Life's a raucous, laughing dance!

Petals of Peculiarity in Bloom

In gardens where the weirdness grows,
Petals shaped like question marks.
Laughter tumbles, throws and flows,
As sunlight dances with the larks.

Colors clash in joyful sprees,
Bees buzz tunes of pure delight.
Nature croons its mysteries,
As the oddities take flight.

Every bloom, a tale to tell,
With roots that chuckle underground.
In this patch where quirks do dwell,
Joy is the only truth we've found.

Amongst the leaves, we strike a pose,
Giggling at life's playful scheme.
In this oddity that glows,
We discover joy in every dream.

Fantasies That Brush Past

In a world where socks dance, lost in their fate,
I ponder on shoes, the odd little trait.
A cat wears a crown, strutting with pride,
While pigeons hold meetings, secrets they hide.

A clock that runs backward, tick-tock goes the sound,
Reminds me of days I'm happily unbound.
A banana in glasses, quite clever and wise,
Keeps smiling at all with its humorous guise.

I sip on my dreams, served fresh from the clouds,
Chewing on laughter, despite all the crowds.
A suitcase of wishes awaits on the shore,
Packed full of punchlines, who could ask for more?

So here's to the quirks that we all seem to share,
Like penguins in bowties or twins with no hair.
Each moment a gem, though it might seem absurd,
A circus of life, and we're all just the herd.

Secrets Whispers Between Laughs

In a garden of giggles where flowers look shocked,
I find little fairies in tea shops, they talked.
With crumpets in hand, they served jokes with a grin,
And toast to the moments we're all trapped within.

A dog with a monocle reads daily old news,
As squirrels trade secrets, wearing their best shoes.
Fish swap their tales of grand journeys and strife,
While ants plan a parade—what a wonderful life!

Each hiccup, a song, and each sneeze a surprise,
The world's painted bright with laughter in disguise.
I watch a balloon float—what dreams must it weave,
Holding on to the secrets we all can believe.

Giraffes play chess in the shade of a tree,
Counting their moves with the utmost glee.
And here I sit sipping my wittiest brew,
Sharing my laughter, my secrets with you.

Curious Echoes of the Everyday

Dancing socks on a lonely floor,
A spoon that thinks it's a spaceship's door.
Cats in hats, plotting to take flight,
Are they stars, or just lost in the night?

Jellybeans in a congress of dreams,
Debating the value of ice cream themes.
Silly pigeons dance on a wire,
While the toaster hums, a concert choir.

If life's a jest, who wrote the play?
A frog in a tutu steals the day.
Chasing shadows with a candy cane,
What was I doing? Oh, never mind the brain!

A rubber chicken sings in the rain,
Echoing laughter, joy mixed with pain.
Through the chaos, a giggle shines bright,
Painting the world in delightfully light.

Fragments of Forgotten Fantasies

A squirrel in shades, reading the news,
While a goldfish dreams of living in shoes.
This cosmic circus is hard to believe,
Between a lost sock and an old piece of weave.

Unicorns munch on spaghetti and peas,
Monkeys juggle muffins with elegant ease.
The moon throws a party, wearing a bow,
And the stars help with the confetti throw.

Tick-tock goes the clock with a wink,
How does it know when to dance or to think?
An octopus tap-dances on a beach,
While mermaids laugh, just out of reach.

On a rollercoaster made of light,
Riding dreams till the morning bright.
Flying cows paint the sky with glee,
Wonders await for you and me.

Puzzles on a Twisted Path

A flower queries why it's a bloom,
While a cactus conspires to craft a room.
This garden tells secrets, filled with mirth,
As squirrels seek wisdom, debating their worth.

Rubber ducks ponder the meaning of life,
In a world where each moment is rife.
Cream pies thrown by nostalgic clowns,
Filling the air with soft giggles and frowns.

Giraffes in top hats playing charades,
While time slips away in a catnip parade.
Jigsaw pieces shaped like dreams,
Are nonsense puzzles of wobbly themes.

A snail races past on the road so wide,
Chasing a lollipop, oh what a ride!
In a realm where laughter is forever in sight,
We'll dance on the edge of the day and night.

The Incongruity of Existence

A penguin in a tux at a beachside rave,
Builds sandcastles where the dolphins wave.
Chocolate rain falls on a lemon tree,
And the goldfish crowns a new king bee.

Ovens bake wishes, soft and warm,
While the moon grins, free from the norm.
Crickets recite plays in the balmy night,
As lightning bugs blink the stage lights bright.

A bear in a bowler hat rides a bike,
Singing to flowers as they take a hike.
Clouds float by like marshmallows sweet,
Dancing through time on ephemeral feet.

Between the giggles and whimsical sighs,
Frogs in formation sing under the skies.
Life's a quirky, delightful jest,
Full of puzzles where we're all guests.

Conundrums of Clockwork

Ticking tock, a watch does sing,
Winding up the silly things.
Chasing time like a fleet-footed hare,
While minutes dance without a care.

A pendulum swings, a beat so neat,
Laughing at those who can't find their feet.
Time is a thief with a wry little grin,
Taking the moments, but where to begin?

Clocks run wild in a whimsical race,
Each second's a reason to giggle with grace.
Days blend together like jumbled yarn,
As we try to remember a life full of charm.

Round and round, we're caught in the spin,
Life's quirky turns, a wild little grin.
Maybe it's fun, this whirling spree,
To find laughter in the clockwork's decree.

Days Spun from Silly String

Waking up with a hair of spaghetti,
Tangled dreams, thoughts all heady.
Pajamas dance while breakfast skips,
Mimicking the joy in our morning trips.

Coffee spills like stories told,
A splash of chaos, a cup of bold.
Time to work, but what's the rush?
In silly string days, we giggle and hush.

Every errand's a whimsical ride,
With ducks in bow ties, our silly guide.
At the grocery store, we twirl with glee,
Cartwheeling through aisles, just you and me.

Sunset paints the sky neon bright,
Endings are funny, but hold on tight.
Life swings like a swing, so carefree,
Days spun from string, forever we'll be.

Echoes of Eccentricity

Echoes bounce off the walls so strange,
Chasing silly thoughts in a wild range.
Rubber chickens squawk in laughter's embrace,
As sanity takes a comical space.

Odd socks mingle in a dance so bizarre,
Mismatched lives, like a shooting star.
Chasing rainbows in mismatched shoes,
Finding delight in the things we choose.

Talk to the moon, it grins back wide,
Hiccups of joy on this whimsical ride.
Cupcakes sprout wings and take to the sky,
With sprinkles of happiness, oh me, oh my!

So here's to the echoes of peculiar cheer,
In a world that's nutty, let's persevere.
Laughter is the thread that weaves through the day,
In our own quirky symphony, we'll endlessly play.

The Dance of Disillusionment

In a land of dreams where socks are lost,
We pirouette through the chaos, no matter the cost.
Fridges play music, and walls hum a tune,
As the sun winks down and chuckles at noon.

Frogs in tuxedos hold a soirée tonight,
Boogieing boldly in the moon's silver light.
Crickets in top hats, all teaching the steps,
To a dance where reality giggles and preps.

In this spin of laughter, we wander and twirl,
Embracing the nonsense as life starts to swirl.
A jab at the normal, with pies in the face,
In this dance of the odd, we all find our place.

So join in the fun, let your spirit ignite,
With each clumsy step, make laughter your light.
For in every tumble and whimsical fall,
We find joy in the dance, we are part of it all.

Searching for Logic in a Madcap World

In a swirl where pigeons plot,
And squirrels wear tiny hats,
I chase the maps that time forgot,
While wondering where my phone's at.

The clock ticks backwards, oh what a feat,
Dogs bark in perfect rhyme,
Raindrops dance to a jazzy beat,
As I search for reason in this crime.

A cat gives me wise old looks,
As I trip over mismatched shoes,
I scribble notes in dusty books,
For answers I dare not lose.

But laughter bubbles in the air,
Twisting meaning into jest,
Turns out life's just a wacky fair,
And joy is seen as the best quest.

Wonders Behind Closed Doors

Behind closed doors, the laughter swells,
Where socks and dreams run free,
Monkeys juggle, wearing bells,
The fridge speaks hilarity.

A tea party with tots in hats,
Unicorns sip on tea,
While grandmas dance with hooting bats,
In this mad little jubilee.

Books recite their wildest plots,
As shadows draw and tease,
Lost in tales of tangled knots,
Where nothing is as it seems, please.

So here's to wonders held so dear,
And giggles through the cracks,
In every door, there's joy, I fear,
Life's whimsy never lacks.

Wading Through Whirlwinds of Thought

Thoughts like tumbleweeds behave,
Rolling through my busy mind,
Chasing clouds that softly wave,
In storms of giggles intertwined.

A sandwich sings a tuneful song,
While pickles dance with glee,
I ponder if it all feels wrong,
Or is it just me being free?

I scribble down my jumbled muse,
On napkins, scraps, and dreams,
Where logic wears an old pair of shoes,
And upside-down's all that redeems.

So here I float in zany tides,
With bubbles made of cheer,
In whirlwinds where a heart abides,
And leaves behind all fear.

The Ridiculousness of Routine

I wake to find a sock parade,
That marches right on by,
While coffee brews in grand charade,
With whispers that make me sigh.

The toast declares it wants to fly,
As eggs juggle a bold dare,
I tiptoe past the cat's sly eye,
Lost in whims that fill the air.

My office chair transforms to dance,
As deadlines swirl in jest,
Turning panic into prance,
Life plays its silly quest.

So mundane's a silly game,
With laughter on each beat,
Embrace the quirks, and hold the flame,
In routines that feel so sweet.

The Clock Ticks Backward

Time's march is a dance, quite bizarre,
With clocks that giggle and whisper ajar.
Minutes retreat like shy little mice,
While seconds tumble, oh, isn't that nice?

Each hour laughs at the pivotal fate,
Sipping tea with fate at a curious rate.
While past meets the future in dubious jest,
Every tick is a riddle, a comical quest.

Beneath a moon that glows upside down,
People wear smiles, but frown like a clown.
Days blend together, a jigsaw in flight,
Finding joy in the strangeness of night.

So we'll dance with confusion, not miss a beat,
In this wacky waltz, life offers a treat.
Like socks that forget how to match and align,
Let's embrace the wild, absurd, and divine.

Quandaries in a Coffee Cup

A cup of coffee full of strange thoughts,
Swirling mysteries, should I sip or not?
Do dreams brew gently or bubble and rise?
In this mug of chaos, I ponder the skies.

The spoon stirs arguments, the cream debates,
What's real in these frothy caffeinated states?
Each sip a conundrum of grand existential force,
I stir and I ponder, the questions endorse.

Shall I worry about sugars or sweetened fate?
Or just gaze in the cup, where reflections await?
A splash of caffeine, a dash of delight,
Oh, to savor the riddles that dance in the night.

So here in this mug, where mysteries swirl,
I laugh with my latte, in giggles I twirl.
The universe whispers, quirky and grand,
In this dizzying cup, life's folly is planned.

Illusions in the Mirror

A glance in the glass reveals wonders profound,
Where my hair is a lion and my smile astounds.
Reflection's a trickster, a jester in guise,
Showing me visions and wild, swirling lies.

Who's that, I wonder, pretending to be,
A version of me—so peculiar, you see?
With eyebrows like rainbows and thoughts like a kite,
The mirror just winks, then fades out of sight.

I grin at the stranger with mismatched shoes,
As we share laughter in this playful ruse.
We argue quite loudly, 'Who's truly the best?'
In this funny duel, I'm far from distressed.

So cheers to the glass that bends space and time,
The absurdity there feels almost like rhyme.
With each silly glance, I redefine me,
In a world full of mirrors, we're bound to be free.

Chasing Shadows of Meaning

In the park where shadows play peek-a-boo,
I chased a thought, but it vanished too soon.
"Hey, come back!" I called to the flickering shade,
But meanings evade like a jigsaw parade.

The trees giggle softly, whispers in air,
While I trip over metaphors, lost in despair.
What's the meaning of grass, or the height of a tree?
They giggle in sunlight, just laughing at me.

A squirrel gives pride to this quest of the night,
As reasons dissolve like stars out of sight.
Am I searching for wisdom or just for a snack?
Chasing shadows of meaning, no path to unpack.

So I dance with my thoughts, like sprites in a dream,
With no goal in mind, just the joyous theme.
For in this wild world, we all take a stand,
Chasing laughter forever, hand in hand.

When Laughter Meets the Void

A chicken crossed the road today,
To question fate, or so they say.
The cars just honked, they weren't aware,
Of all the jokes left in the air.

A jester danced upon the brink,
Of life's great stage and took a drink.
He tossed his hat toward the sun,
And laughed because we're all just one.

The void replied with silent glee,
"Why so serious? Just be free!"
So off he went, a silly spree,
With nothing left but irony.

In shadows deep where nonsense grows,
A laughter tree in chaos glows.
It whispers truths we often hide,
When life's a joke, enjoy the ride.

Pondering the Peculiar Pathways

A snail decided on a race,
With a cheetah in a silly chase.
They pondered deep, the end was clear,
Both agreed, it's all mere cheer.

The grass grew tall, the clouds all laughed,
In this strange game, they split the craft.
Time held still while they debated,
Who sighed louder, and who was fated.

A toadstool dressed in polka dots,
Hid secrets deep in tangled knots.
With every twist, a giggle sprout,
Life's mysteries, they laugh about.

So down the path, they spun and twirled,
While pondering why the world is swirled.
In every step, a little jest,
That life's a puzzle, badly dressed.

Symphony of the Unseen

A drumstick played an awkward beat,
While elephants danced with shoeless feet.
A melody that made no sense,
Yet filled the air with sweet suspense.

Orchestras of cats in wooly hats,
Conducted by a flock of bats.
A symphony of woeful sighs,
And all the joy it just implies.

The flautist was a bumblebee,
Buzzing notes of sheer jubilee.
The world applauded, unaware,
That music thrived on pure despair.

Yet laughter rang where silence wept,
In melodies the lost ones kept.
For in chaos, harmony gleams,
And nonsense sings of our wild dreams.

Jesters in the Garden of Chaos

Two jesters pranced in vibrant shoes,
Twirled in circles, spreading news.
They planted seeds of goofy glee,
In gardens where the wild things be.

Bright flowers bloomed in technicolor,
Mocking logic like no other.
They laughed as bees played jumpy games,
While petals whispered silly names.

Amidst the weeds, a pot of gold,
Stood proudly, claiming to be bold.
But in its shine, a riddle grew,
That life's a jest, and we're the clue.

So here we bloom in guffawing light,
In chaos found, our hearts take flight.
For every giggle hides a truth,
In this strange dance of ancient youth.

Fragments of Joy in a Dissonant World

In a world where socks disappear,
We dance with mismatched feet,
Laughter echoes in the void,
As we stumble to the beat.

A cat yells at the moon,
As if it stole her prize,
Birds wear tiny hats and bow,
With an air of grand surprise.

We chase down rainbows made of cheese,
Only to find them fake,
But on our way, a giggle blooms,
In the laughter that we make.

So here's to joy in chaos loud,
And quirks that paint our days,
We'll toast to all the little things,
That life mocks in playful ways.

Curiosities in a Hall of Mirrors

In a hall where reflections grin,
We ponder if we're real,
The mirrors giggle back at us,
As we question what we feel.

A dapper ghost in polka dots,
Turns and tips his hat,
While shadows dance with jellybeans,
In a waltz that's oh-so-flat.

If I step left, will I meet myself?
Or is that just a trick?
The walls are filled with questions loud,
Though answers come in quick.

So we spin around in merry glee,
In this maze of playful doubt,
For every bend, a chuckle found,
In the absurdity we tout.

Kaleidoscopic Dreams in a Gray Reality

In a world of dull and muted tones,
I dream in technicolor hues,
Where unicorns roam with pink balloons,
And laughter is the morning news.

Bananas wear pajamas here,
We skip upon the clouds,
A fish rides by on roller skates,
And sings in cheerful crowds.

The sun throws pancakes from the sky,
While trees play chess with squirrels,
And everyone just takes a bite,
While dancing with their swirls.

So let us toast to dreamers bold,
Who color every gray,
With whims that tickle our minds' eye,
In this peculiar ballet.

The Art of Tripping Over Meaning

In the art gallery of thoughts,
I trip on frames of doubt,
They're filled with wild interpretations,
That make us twist and shout.

A painting speaks in muffled tones,
As we scrutinize its stare,
We question if it's art at all,
Or maybe just despair.

The sculptor shapes a crumpled note,
That whispers, "I'm not sure,"
We laugh because we'd understand,
If we could just endure.

So let us stumble through our fears,
With laughter as our guide,
For every trip reveals a truth,
In the absurdity we bide.

Beneath Stars That Mock Us

Beneath the sky of twinkling eyes,
We laugh at fate as it slyly sighs.
A dance of chaos in cosmic spree,
The stars wink down, as if to agree.

Juggling dreams with a rubber chicken,
Life's funny bone seems always stricken.
With each mishap, a chuckle escapes,
As we wear smiles, like silly capes.

We sail on boats with holes so wide,
A circus act on the cosmic tide.
Cackling clowns in our veins do play,
Turning mundane into cabaret.

In the theater of life, we prance and twirl,
With the universe shaping our wild whirl.
Underneath stars that chuckle and tease,
We revel in joy, life's oddities please.

Fluid Dreams and Fractured Realities

Dreams slip through fingers like sand so fine,
Floating on whims like bubbles in brine.
Reality twists in a jester's grin,
We giggle as we spiral, dive, and spin.

With each dawn we play a game of chance,
To tango with fate in a slapstick dance.
The world's a stage of peculiar sights,
Where everything's funny, nothing ignites.

Thoughts weave and wobble like jelly on plates,
Chasing absurdities through crooked gates.
In this theatre, we're all but fools,
Reveling in chaos, breaking all rules.

So float with me on this laughable stream,
As we surf the tides of a fractured dream.
Each day's a farce, with laughter, we cope,
In fluid moments, we find our hope.

The Gravity of Lightheartedness

In a world that spins like a dizzy top,
We soar through giggles, never to stop.
With balloons as hearts, we drift so high,
Finding comfort in a wink from the sky.

Bouncing on whims like a rubber band,
We dance on dreams, not quite as planned.
Every misstep styled with flair,
As gravity pulls us, we twirl in air.

Here, nonsense reigns with a crown so bright,
We toast to silliness, hearts full of light.
Through the chaos, we chase the grace,
Finding joy in every ridiculous space.

So let's flip the world on its funny side,
In laughter and mirth, we gladly abide.
The heart's a kite in a playful breeze,
In lighthearted moments, we find our ease.

Bowties and Bizarre Quandaries

In bowties askew and socks of pink,
We ponder the life we barely think.
A riddle wrapped in a joke so rare,
Strange quandaries float in the brisk air.

Why do penguins waddle in a parade?
Why does sunshine think it should invade?
Questions tumble, like grapes in a vat,
Filling our days with the "what if" spat.

With rubber ducks as our sage advisors,
We wade through puddles, grin like risers.
Every oddball thought a treasure trove,
Life's quirks are what we most approve.

So raise a glass to the whims we chase,
In bowties and laughter, we find our place.
Embracing the bizarre in joyful cheers,
Finding delight in our zany years.

The Zen of a Twisted Mind

In a world of upside-down, I spin my thoughts,
Chasing shadows through the sunny spots.
Why do we laugh when the punchline's late?
Life's a strange puzzle, let's contemplate.

A rubber chicken in a boardroom's grace,
Silly antics in a solemn place.
When sense is lost, we dance and twirl,
Like a dervish love in a cartwheel whirl.

I search for wisdom in a lava lamp,
While socks converse, making sense of their camp.
A toaster sings, while bread's being fried,
In this odd ballet, let joy be our guide.

So let's embrace the quirks, have a jest,
With wobbly logic, we surely are blessed.
In giggles and chuckles, we find our way,
Through this topsy-turvy cabaret.

Confetti in the Pockets of Time

Time flies with glitter, stuck to our shoes,
Moments like confetti, bright but diffuse.
Each second a dancer that twirls on a whim,
Elusive like dreams that flicker and dim.

An hourglass tumbles with jellybeans inside,
Tick-tock, tick-tock, on a carnival ride.
What if clouds wore hats, just for the thrill?
And rain played jazz while the sun took a chill?

Life's a game show with no final round,
With eggplant emojis in the lost-and-found.
Each twist and turn a circus of glee,
In the pockets of time, we're wild and free.

So gather your sparkles, hold them up high,
Make wishes on giggles, let worries fly.
With confetti moments, we'll charm the breeze,
Dancing through life with a wink and a tease.

Cartwheeling Through the Grand Illusion

I cartwheel through scenes where logic runs thin,
Where cats wear sunglasses and grasses are green.
Life's a funhouse mirror, reflecting quite strange,
A kaleidoscope world that likes to derange.

Pizza-shaped clouds in a peach-colored sky,
We'll surf on the giggles and let worries sigh.
Why walk when you can tumble and spin,
In this carefree dance, let the chaos begin!

Chasing a dream on a pogo stick,
Frogs in bowties doing a magic trick.
The clock strikes twelve, and the make-believe starts,
With unicorns tap dancing in our hearts.

So take a leap into this circus of cheer,
Where every wild notion is welcome here.
In the grand illusion, we find our way,
With a skip and a swoop, let's seize the day!

The Sunshine in a Sideways Rain

When raindrops giggle and puddles sing,
We skip under umbrellas that got lost in the spring.
Why frown at the clouds in such a merry display,
When rainbows are cheeky, just a hop away?

With sunshine sideways, life takes a turn,
Each drop is a spark, watch the laughter churn.
Silly hats on ducks, they waddle and sway,
In this flip-flop weather, we dance and play.

The sun spills its joy in golden refrains,
As trees share secrets with the whimsical rains.
A breeze full of giggles tickles the leaves,
In the sideways sunshine, we find what we believe.

So let's toast to puddles and skies that gleam,
In this merry madness, let's dream our dream.
With a wink from the universe, let laughter reign,
In the happy chaos of sideways rain.

The Paradoxical Parade

Clowns juggle with fate, oh what a sight,
While elephants tiptoe under the moonlight.
A lion wears glasses, reads the news,
And the audience wonders, what's real to choose?

Balloons whisper secrets, a comic affair,
The tightrope dancer jumps, without a care.
Penguins in tuxedos, they waddle and sway,
As the drummer beats rhythm, in a fruity ballet.

A jester shouts riddles, their punchlines collide,
While unicorns prance in a hesitant stride.
What a delightful circus of whims and screams,
Where logic is tangled in cotton candy dreams.

So join the procession, with chuckles and cheer,
Life is the joke, let's laugh till we tear.
In this whimsical chaos, we dance and play,
Sipping on laughter, come join the bouquet.

A Tapestry of Tangles

Threads of confusion in a colorful weave,
Stitched by the whims that we hardly perceive.
A sock and a sandwich share a secret toast,
While time takes a break, just to make space for ghosts.

Cats in bow ties debate politics grand,
While squirrels compete in a ballet so planned.
Rabbits wear watches, the minutes unwind,
In a garden where roses and riddles are blind.

The sun spills its paint on the canvas of bees,
As carrots discuss with the birds in the trees.
What's patience? A question that's woven so tight,
In the loom of our laughter, absurdly polite.

Each day is a patch with a story to tell,
In this quilt of life's questions, we giggle and dwell.
Frogs croak in the night, rhyming with stars,
In this tapestry tangled with humorous scars.

Questions in a World of Answers

Why does the toaster dance while it toasts?
And what makes the moon so good at its boasts?
The mug on the shelf claims it's coffee time,
While spoons hum a tune, an absurd little rhyme.

Is grass greener when cows wear sunglasses?
Or do they just pose, dodging life's impasses?
What do shadows do when the sun takes a break?
Whisper sweet nothings to the mischief they make?

A fish wrote a novel on navigating tides,
While starfish critique, with their many-eyed guides.
Do trees speculate on their home in the breeze?
In a world filled with questions, we chuckle with ease.

As answers orbit like planets so vast,
We giggle at truths that slip through so fast.
Join in the laughter, let curious minds twirl,
In this collection of questions, we spin and swirl.

Nonsense Wrapped in Poetry

A pickle in a bowler hat struts down the lane,
While jellybeans chatter about love and pain.
A snail sips on tea from a dainty fine cup,
As the sun asks a cloud, 'Why don't you light up?'

The moon wears pajamas, all polka-dotted so bright,
While stars swap their stories in the stillness of night.
A bicycle giggles, riding on air,
As the leaves whisper nonsense without any care.

Frogs march in rhythm, wearing tiny neat boots,
While grasshoppers play with the sound of flutes.
A cat in a hammock pretends to be wise,
While dreaming of fish tales and pie in the skies.

Nonsense is woven in every soft line,
Where laughter and whimsy do merrily twine.
Join the circus of words, let your heart take a flight,
In this silly dimension, let's laugh through the night.

The Enigma of Everyday Nonsense

Why do socks vanish in the wash?
As if they live in a sock-ditch swash.
My cat plots world domination, I swear,
While I search for lost keys with despair.

Lunch breaks turn into grand adventures,
With sandwiches making bold indentures.
The coffee machine needs a diploma,
To brew my dreams and not just aroma.

Why do we dance in the grocery aisle?
As shoppers gaze, all lost in a smile.
Life's little quirks spin us round in glee,
Like juggling tomatoes, carefree and free.

Tomorrow's plans are scribbled in chalk,
While we trip over mismatched socks on our walk.
Yet still we laugh at the comic routine,
In this circus called life, absurd but serene.

A Dialogue with Daffodils

Daffodils whisper secrets to the breeze,
While I ask them, 'Have you lost your keys?'
They chuckle and sway, petals in delight,
As I ponder my lunch choices in twilight.

Birds argue loudly about their next song,
While I gaze at their antics, it feels wrong.
Is it nature's jest or a jest of mine?
Either way, I chuckle over green vine.

Why do squirrels hoard popcorn in trees?
As if planning a feast to appease.
Yet I'm here, baffled by a sandwich's fate,
Wondering if ketchup can make it first-rate.

Oh, life's gentle folly with flowers in tow,
As I seek a meaning only the daisies know.
And still, we share laughter in gardens bright,
A chat with the blooms in the soft evening light.

Wonders of Whimsy That Spin

In the land of socks, where patterns collide,
Strange creatures laugh as they take a ride.
The toaster sings tunes of burnt bread in jest,
As I munch on leftovers, pondering the quest.

Penguins in tuxedos strut down the street,
Chasing their dreams on whimsical feet.
Each sidewalk a stage, where laughter erupts,
In this nonsensical dance, we're all corrupt.

Forget about clocks; they tick at their whim,
Which hour to take? There's no rule of them.
Yet here I am, lost in the clock's tattle,
While jellybeans compete in silly battle.

Clouds play dress-up in whimsical shade,
While I trip over thoughts that won't seem to fade.
In this world of wonder, absurd and bright,
I'll sit with the nonsense, and savor the light.

The Comet's Baffling Trail

A comet zooms past, what's its grand plan?
Is it racing the moon, plotting with the sun?
While I stand on my porch, hair blown wild,
Eating stale popcorn like a bewildered child.

Starfish debate on the meaning of dirt,
As I mix my salad with frosting, dessert.
Each planet a punk, strumming cosmic guitar,
Taking bets on how far we each are.

Why do dreams parade like peacocks in night?
Dancing through feelings, refusing to fight.
And though I keep tripping over my shoe lace,
I'll join in the dance with a whimsical grace.

So here's to the mirth that makes us all grin,
In this baffling world where nonsense begins.
With orbits of joy that make hearts entwine,
Today, we are silly, and everything's fine.

When Hiccups Echo in the Abyss

In a void where echoes yelp,
My hiccups dance, a lonely waltz.
Each gasp erupts, a silent help,
While shadows giggle and convulse.

The abyss hums with laughter strange,
As time forgets my muted screams.
A hiccup here, a hiccup range,
Life's punchline slips from all my dreams.

I clasp the air with hopeful hands,
But find it slippery and sly.
Jokes unmade in endless sands,
And all I do is wonder why.

Still, I giggle with the night,
For nonsensical is this jest.
As hiccups fade, so dims the light,
While I lay down, a fool at rest.

Thoughts That Tangle and Twist

My mind's a cat with yarn to play,
It pounces on each whimsical thread.
A tangle here leads thoughts astray,
As logic spins, the chaos spreads.

I ponder deep, like fish in tanks,
Then surface for a silly gasp.
My thoughts cartwheel, give me frank,
Life's wacky truth, a jester's clasp.

With every twist, I laugh aloud,
Confusion's fog, a muffled cheer.
In tangled webs, I find a crowd,
Where nonsense reigns, the vision's clear.

And as I swim in thoughts askew,
A tickle stirs beneath my skin.
In twisting depths, I start anew,
Embracing knots where I begin.

Beliefs in a Bag of Marbles

I carry round a bag of dreams,
Each marble clinks with hope and glee.
But gravity might tear its seams,
And scatter truths like leaves in spree.

Some marbles shine with colors bold,
Others dull, as whispers fade.
In this bag, mysteries unfold,
Yet who can speak of truths we've made?

I toss them high, they plop and roll,
A game of chance with fate I play.
Each marble holds a fractured soul,
Beliefs collide and drift away.

In every drop, I find delight,
With clanking sounds of silly fate.
These marbles' paths, as day meets night,
A bag of dreams, a playful state.

Painting with Time's Unruly Brush

With colors bold and strokes askew,
I paint my days, a canvas wild.
The hues of laughter, gray and blue,
Amidst the chaos, I'm a child.

Time's brush drips with candor bright,
Blotting out reason with each sweep.
A masterpiece of pure delight,
Where nonsense thrives and echoes leap.

I dip and swirl with reckless flare,
Creating scenes that twist and twirl.
Each daub a sigh, a laugh, a prayer,
In life's mad art, I freely whirl.

So let me paint with all my might,
Each brushstroke sketches foolish grace.
In every clash of dark and light,
I find the absurdity's embrace.

Journeying Through a Field of Whimsy

In fields where rabbits wear their shoes,
They dance with squirrels, spinning clues.
The sun is laughing, clouds in disguise,
While trees gossip in cheerful sighs.

A dog with glasses reads a book,
As flowers nod and shadows look.
Each breeze offers a ticklish tease,
Where moments linger like buzzing bees.

The butterflies make witty remarks,
While frogs play chess on lily parks.
With every step, the grass will sing,
In this peculiar, merry thing.

So join the fest, don't miss the fun,
Beneath the stars, away we run.
Life's a carnival, a silly spree,
In this odd, whimsical jubilee.

Life's Playful Paradox

The cat meows like it's Shakespeare's play,
While I wonder what dogs would say.
Juggling tasks with a grin so wide,
Spilling coffee, but what a ride!

Time ticks backward, or maybe it's lore,
As socks refuse to stay in their drawer.
The moon winks down, a cheeky sprite,
While clocks tick-tock in the quiet night.

Chasing shadows of things long gone,
My sandwich melts, but I move on.
Life's a puzzle with missing parts,
Made of laughter and quirky arts.

So here's to the chaos, the playful spins,
Where folly dances and laughter wins.
Drifting through this nonsensical maze,
We'll find our joy in humorous ways.

Reflections from a Bouncing Ball

A bouncing ball in a world of dreams,
Flipping and flopping, bursting at seams.
It rolls through puddles of jittery cheer,
With every leap, absurdity near.

The ground is bumpy, yet I glide,
Past gnomes playing hopscotch, side by side.
With each bounce, a giggle's released,
In this arena, we're all a feast.

Clouds become marshmallows, fluffy and sweet,
As I bounce onward, weaving my feet.
Laughter bubbles in this curious space,
A carnival ride with a cheeky face.

So let me bounce till the day's all through,
On paths where dreams and folly brew.
Life's a game, come join the throng,
In the rhythm of the silly song.

Lullabies of the Unraveling Mind

Whispers of thoughts like tangled yarn,
A cat naps softly on a field of barn.
The clouds play chess with the sun above,
As shadows waltz, we fall in love.

Dreams do cartwheels, teasing the day,
While clocks melt down in a comical play.
It's all a jest, the mind's dance hall,
Where logic tumbles like a rolling ball.

Riddles wrap around common sense,
As laughter echoes in each pretense.
We hum lullabies to the silly scene,
In this garden where nothing's routine.

So rest your thoughts on a cloud-shaped bed,
In this pandemonium, joy's widespread.
As winks and grins fill the silent slide,
We find sweet comfort in the joyful ride.

Chronicles of Delightful Confusion

In a world where socks seem to stray,
And spoons have secret meetings each day,
The cat speaks fluent Spanish, no doubt,
While pots conspire with pans to shout.

A dance of chaos on charred toast,
Where rabbits plot their wildest boast,
And every umbrella's a sneak attack,
As rain falls sideways, never lack.

Juggling oranges, a baker's task,
With sticky fingers, one dares to ask,
Why pancakes fly and kitchen timers sing,
In this feast of folly, who'd be king?

So here we bustle, in hats askew,
Chasing butterflies that seem to woo,
Life's a riddle, wrapped in jest,
In confusion's arms, we find our rest.

The Carnival of Broken Dreams

Balloons float high, but some are deflated,
Clowns with laughter, yet they're frustrated,
The Ferris wheel spins in crooked delight,
While popcorn chats into the night.

A tightrope walker wobbles with glee,
His shadow plays tricks, elusive as tea,
The ringmaster juggles woes like fire,
As dreams dissolve in the cotton candy mire.

A duck in boots quacks a profound tune,
While juggling jellybeans under the moon,
Life's merry-go-round, a dizzying show,
With every spin, we forget what we know.

So grab your ticket, the ride's never clear,
In laughter and confusion, there's much to cheer,
For in this carnival, tales intertwine,
In broken dreams, we find our spine.

Musings from the Edge of Sanity

A hat that talks, oh what a sight,
It tells me jokes in the dead of night,
While clocks march backward, to my surprise,
And fish wear glasses, oh how they rise!

With whims like jelly, and thoughts like soup,
I ride my bicycle through a goat-filled group,
The trees all whisper of secrets untold,
As squirrels recite sonnets, bold.

In this realm of nonsense, I find my path,
As rainbows squabble and sunlight hath,
A way of dancing in shoes too tight,
And reveling in shadows that twirl with fright.

So if you find me on this ledge,
With scribbled thoughts, like a crazy pledge,
Join my parade, we'll laugh in glee,
On the edge of sanity, wild and free.

Bask in the Quicksand Sunshine

In quicksand warmth, we sink with smiles,
As sunshine giggles and plays in styles,
The world winks back with a cheeky cheer,
As daisies nod and whisper near.

A marathon of turtles, oh what a race,
Chasing the leaves that dance in space,
The sun plays tricks, like a mischievous cat,
While butterflies ponder where they're at.

Each glance reveals a curious case,
Of rabbits that wear a polka dot brace,
And silence shouts in a bustling din,
Where laughter tumbles, let's begin!

So here we bask in the shining sand,
With logic lost, we dare to stand,
In the warmth of laughter, we find our fun,
In quicksand sunshine, where life's on the run.

Chasing the Flickering Fireflies

In twilight's glow, they dart like thoughts,
Chasing shadows in zigzag plots.
A jar of dreams, oh what a race,
With wings so bright, they mock our pace.

We stumble on grass, lost in the flick,
While giggles erupt, our legs going thick.
It's a circus of lights, an absurd ballet,
In this goofy dance, we'll lose our way.

With jars held high, we capture hopes,
Yet, empty hands teach better ropes.
For life's little bugs lead wobbly trails,
In a jar of laughter, our joy prevails.

So catch that glow, it won't stick around,
With every heart thump, the night's profound.
We laugh as we grasp, yet none remain,
In the chase for the fireflies, who's really insane?

Riddles Beneath the Surface

The world spins round with questions deep,
Like turtles in teacups, they quietly seep.
Why do socks vanish in the wash?
An enigma wrapped in a laundry squosh.

Beneath the calm, a tempest brews,
Fish wearing hats sing the evening blues.
Why do we stare at clouds overhead?
Waiting for wisdom, yet dread instead!

The mirror laughs as it shows our face,
Reflections of chaos in a crowded space.
We puzzle and ponder with each fleeting hour,
As raindrops tap dance, our brains' power.

In riddles we cradle our daily grind,
With quirk and jest, our sanity's blind.
So toss your questions to the fickle air,
For life's delightful mysteries await our care.

Mirth in the Melancholy

A clown in the corner, holding a frown,
Juggles with sorrow while slipping down.
Yet laughter erupts like a pop from a cork,
In the bittersweet glow, we smile and quirk.

Rain drizzles on cakes, frosting soaks through,
Soggy delight, is it life's to undo?
Each slice serves a giggle, an icing-tainted cheer,
In puddles of whimsy, we dance with our fear.

The shadows believe they can hide the glow,
Yet in each corner, bright giggles bestow.
A parade of the silly in blue every day,
With mirth squeezed from tears, we waltz, come what may.

Life's tipsy waltz, a comic affair,
Jests and jabs in the weight of the air.
So sip from your heart, let joy intertwine,
For the funny in sorrow's the best glass of wine!

Snapshots of a Surreal Soiree

In a room of chairs, the cats all converse,
Debating their names like it's art, for the worse.
While teacups do tango, and spoons run wild,
Laughter spills over, unruly and child.

The clock melts away, losing track of the time,
Bubbles float past, singing sweet nursery rhyme.
Each laugh carries dreams on a balloon's gentle sway,
In this odd soirée, we dance 'til the day.

Frogs in tuxedos orchestrate the fun,
While socks postulate how to outrun the sun.
Each glance a snapshot of moments so rare,
As we twirl 'round the whims of this whimsical fair.

So lift up your cups to the strange and divine,
In the circus of life, let your laughter align.
For every oddity holds a wink from the soul,
In snapshots of joy, our quirks make us whole.

Epiphanies from an Open Window

A cat on a roof, surveying the street,
Meowing at pigeons, oh what a feat!
Cars honk and rush, but he takes his time,
Life's a grand joke, a rhythm, a rhyme.

A man with a hat walks two tiny dogs,
They stop for a chat with a couple of frogs.
In moments like these, the world seems to pause,
And laughter erupts, a round of applause.

A child on a swing sings high in the air,
While the wind whispers secrets that few ever share.
The clouds roll above, they dance and they sway,
Life's simple joys are outsmarting the gray.

So let the sun shine, and let the rain fall,
With quirky observations that tickle us all.
An open window frames this silly delight,
Where whimsy and wonder make everything bright.

The Unraveling Thread

A sock has a hole that leads to a dream,
Where mismatched pawns plot a buttercream scheme.
Time flows like yarn, with knots here and there,
It's all a grand tapestry woven with flair.

A toaster rebelliously spits out its bread,
While the kettle begins its long-winded thread.
Chairs gossip in corners, they lean and they sway,
Cackling about how we waste half the day.

The plants sing in whispers, their leaves all aglow,
As the fridge hums a tune, a soft, steady flow.
Each odd little moment adds colors and shades,
In the fabric of life, there's laughter that fades.

So what if the sun isn't always in sight?
Joy hides in the corners, just waiting for light.
Follow the thread, let it dance all around,
In the chaos of life, sweet chuckles abound.

Portraits of a Whimsical Universe

An elephant walks in a tutu of pink,
While zebras debate, and the owls simply wink.
Stars in the sky wear glasses so round,
They read comic books, chuckling without sound.

A tree has a hat that it wears all day,
As squirrels plan picnics in their own silly way.
The moon winks back with a silvery grin,
While time tick-tocks with a playful spin.

With fish on scooters, zooming through air,
And clouds made of candy that float without care,
Each portrait a moment, a splash of delight,
In this whimsical world, everything's right.

In laughter's embrace, we twirl and we spin,
As life paints its canvas, let the giggles begin.
Amidst cosmic jests and humor divine,
We sip all the whimsy, and life is just fine.

Laughter Between the Raindrops

A duck in a puddle declares it a plus,
While people with umbrellas look quite nonplussed.
The rain has a rhythm, a soft little dance,
A chance for silliness, a whimsical chance.

There's splashing and giggling that fills up the air,
As children embrace the wetness without care.
Each droplet a note in a quirky refrain,
Conducting a symphony, light-hearted and plain.

A snail on parade wears a crown made of leaf,
While clouds roll on by with a mock disbelief.
The sun sneaks a peek, plays hide-and-seek,
And laughter erupts from a sky that's so bleak.

So hop like a frog, wear your rain boots with glee,
Let the droplets fall down, set the spirit free.
In the chaos of weather, let joy have its say,
For life is a jest wrapped in folly and play.

Whirlwinds of Thought in a Still Room

In a room where silence reigns,
Thoughts spin like wild, loose reins.
Clock ticks loud, a teasing trick,
Each second laughs, then runs quick.

Dust motes dance in sunbeam light,
Chasing shadows, what a sight!
A chair squeaks out a sobbing sigh,
While walls conspire, oh my, oh my!

Pencils roll like runaway cars,
Erasers hide behind sofa bars.
Laughter echoes in empty space,
Fun high jinks in this quiet place!

Yet stillness holds a curious grin,
As thoughts race by like a whirlwind spin.
The ordinary turns quite absurd,
In this realm where silence is heard.

Balancing Acts on a Tightrope of Uncertainty

Walking on a string so thin,
Wobbling like a bottle of gin.
The ground below, a waiting trap,
Each step a chance for a muddy slap.

A jester's hat flops on my head,
While the crowd just stares instead.
I juggle cats, oh what a fright,
Hoping they don't take to flight!

Balloons twist under my chin,
Floating dreams, where to begin?
A tumble here could spark a laugh,
But gravity loves a photograph.

Yet on this rope, I learn to sway,
Each wobble is a brand new play.
Life's a circus, wild and bright,
A thrilling ride, oh what a sight!

Whispers of a Wondrous Nonsense

Gobbledygook swirls in the breeze,
Words that giggle, as they tease.
A rabbit with a clock on its back,
Sips tea from a saucer, but what's the lack?

Dancing spoons sing lullabies,
While toasters plot under sunny skies.
Salad hearts wear tiny crowns,
Joking with the leafy gowns.

Whispers float like cotton candy,
In a world that feels so dandy.
Eggs that paint themselves with grace,
In this odd, delightful place.

Each bizarre thought flutters high,
Like butterflies that kiss the sky.
Embrace the quirks, let out the giggles,
In this magical whirl of wiggles!

Dancing on the Edge of Reason

On the ledge of logic, I sway,
With a tutu made of hay.
A serenade of silly songs,
Where the oddbirds sing along.

Cows wear caps, and sheep don ties,
As rabbits hold debates and sighs.
The moon peeks through a floppy hat,
As nonsense dances, imagine that!

Stumbling thoughts form quite a line,
As particles of laughter twine.
Each twist and turn, a comic twist,
In the grand ballet of a whimsical list.

So take a leap, and don't be afraid,
Life's absurdities are humorously laid.
In this waltz where reason slips,
Join the dance with joyous quips!

Slices of Life on Paper Plates

Life served warm on a flimsy sheet,
Spaghetti spills and sauce retreats.
Napkin dreams of cleanliness,
While ketchup laughs at our distress.

Forks are fighting for their chance,
As pickles wiggle in a dance.
Banana peels, the jesters' grin,
Slipping wisdom through the din.

Burgers mumble their greasy tales,
In sunlit parks, on windy trails.
A side of fries with witty bite,
In this picnic of pure delight.

Life's a feast of muted hues,
Every flavor here's a ruse.
On paper plates we share our fate,
With laughter thick as cream on cake.

Musings from a Cracked Teacup

A little chip, a tiny flaw,
Holds conversations, breaking law.
Tea leaves swirl in crazy shapes,
As laughter bubbles, hope escapes.

Sippin' wisdom from the edge,
Thoughts tumble forth like a hedge.
Whispers echo in porcelain songs,
While gravity hums and sings along.

Sugar cubes, like dreams, dissolve,
In this riddle, we evolve.
Caution thrown with every sip,
Life's a journey, let it slip.

Cracked and chipped, we pile on cheer,
In every sip, a little sneer.
Life's brew is oddly steeped,
With each misstep, we're more enriched.

Orchestrating the Unthinkable

Bathtubs play in symphony,
Rubber ducks, the key to glee.
Conductors of a soap-bubble dream,
With each pop, the worries seem to stream.

Pans crash like cymbals, a daring feat,
In kitchens where the chaos meets.
Cooking up a tune so wild,
Even spatulas are reconciled.

On the table, forks take a bow,
Knives play bravely, but where, oh where, now?
The recipe strikes a chord so bright,
While the cake explodes in laughter's light.

In this theater of mishaps grand,
Life performs, just give a hand.
As chaos dances, join the beat,
Orchestrate fun, grab a seat!

The Jigsaw of Jests and Jests

Pieces scattered, fun to find,
Edges laughing, quite refined.
The sky, a puzzle filled with cheer,
While upside-down is just the sphere.

Cats and socks, they roll and play,
In missing colors, they display.
A truly mad artist's delight,
As mismatched dreams take flight.

Laughter fills the coffee cup,
As the dog jumps, then gives up.
In this chaos, we're entwined,
Finding joy is what we find.

Life's a game with pieces few,
Yet each odd shape brings a view.
So gather 'round, let's play this quest,
In jigsaw jests, we find our rest.

The Fickle Clock of Human Experience

Time ticks funny, like a cat in socks,
Running in circles, avoiding clocks.
We chase the hours, they scoff and flee,
Minutes are monsters, wild and free.

We plan our days, oh what a joke!
Life's a mad dance, just smoke and smoke.
With every tick, we fumble and fall,
Yet still we giggle, through it all.

Round and round, our dreams take flight,
Chasing sunsets, from day to night.
The clock keeps laughing, what a farce,
Ticking along, breaking our hearts.

But here's the twist, take off your shoes,
Join the parade, it's all yours to lose.
Strike up a tune, let the humor swell,
In this wacky world, we dance so well.

Observing the Ridiculous from the Sidelines

With popcorn in hand, I watch the show,
Life's circus unfolds, complete with a throw.
Clowns in suits, juggling their dreams,
    Falling apart at the seams.

The sun wears shades, the moon takes a dive,
    In this carnival, we're all alive.
Birds in bow ties, squirrels in hats,
Life's a grand stage of absurd chitchats.

People skip, then suddenly freeze,
Pausing to ponder a long string of cheese.
I chuckle and sigh, sipping my drink,
How marvelous to watch, without having to think.

Mimes shout loudly, though no sound escapes,
    Caught up in gestures, like tangled tapes.
Here from the sidelines, it's all quite divine,
A spectacle grand, where the jokes intertwine.

Sipping Tea with a Flying Elephant

In a teacup garden, elephants soar,
With wings made of candy, they glide and explore.
I pour some tea, watch the chaos unfold,
As they sip their dreams, so sweet yet bold.

One twirls in a tutu, another in stripes,
Balancing cupcakes and humorous types.
They giggle and snort, what a sight to behold,
Tea spills on the table, yet never grows cold.

Chai clouds rustle, the air is crisp,
With each little laugh, life does a wisp.
The world turns silly, as reality bends,
In this tea party realm, where laughter transcends.

Floating on marshmallows, we sip and we sway,
In the heart of nonsense, we frolic and play.
With every sweet sip, let your worries flee,
Join in the madness, come sip tea with me.

Puzzles Unsolved on the Shelf of Time

Dusty puzzles sit, waiting for me,
With pieces like thoughts, scattered and free.
The cat walks by, claiming a space,
While I scratch my head in this mystical race.

Each piece is a question, a riddle, a joke,
Finding the edges, it turns out, a cloak.
The image remains a fantastical blur,
Yet I can't help but chuckle, for that's how we were.

What color is laughter? What shape does it take?
I search for the answers, realize it's fake.
Patterns emerge, like a dance on the floor,
As I find where to fit all the odds and the more.

So here's to the puzzles, both silly and grand,
A lifetime of humor, within reach of my hand.
On this shelf of time, let's piece it in fun,
For the answers are scattered, but smiles weigh a ton.

Tumultuous Waves on a Still Sea

The sun smiles wide at the flat blue,
But whispers of trouble in the tide's brew.
Fish wear goggles, laughing at their fuss,
While crabs plot schemes in a salty bus.

Seagulls trade secrets, rolling on the floor,
A jellyfish juggles, what's it all for?
Waves flip-flop thoughts like socks in a dryer,
Each splash is a giggle, fueling the fire.

Splash! There goes a clam with a top hat on,
Polka-dot turtles dance until they're gone.
How strange to see chaos in sunshine's beam,
Yet all of it's silly—perhaps just a dream.

Are we the punchline? A cosmic joke?
Life's a wacky circus, smoke rings of smoke.
Sailors chase rainbows in boats made of cheese,
And waves greet the shore with a chuckle and wheeze.

An Orchestra of Misfit Instruments

Instruments gather, a quirky parade,
With spoons and forks ready to serenade.
A tuba spills notes like spaghetti on plates,
While trumpets salute with twists of their fates.

The violin grumbles, 'I've lost my good bow!'
And the flute just giggles, 'I'll steal the show!'
A cymbal crashes laughing, 'No one can play!'
As the kit of wild sounds joins in the fray.

Banjos strum like they're caught in a spin,
As tambourines rattle, they dance with a grin.
Each note is a misstep, a slip on the stage,
Creating a symphony of comedic rage.

They play on together, no rhythm in sight,
Yet somehow it sparkles, a raucous delight.
When music is chaos, who needs it to rhyme?
The joy is all clever, silliness the prime.

Laughing at the Incomprehensible

Life's a riddle wrapped in a sock,
Each tick of the clock, just a stubborn mock.
People chase answers like children with sweets,
While time sneaks away on mischievous feet.

Questions spiral 'round like wind in a tunnel,
Searching for meaning – oh, isn't it funnell?
We ponder and ponder, our heads in a spin,
And laugh at the puzzles we can't quite begin.

Philosophers wonder while eating their fries,
With gravy on wisdom, it drizzles and flies.
The answers elude like a cat on a chase,
While the world just giggles, smirking in space.

Embrace the absurdity, dance in the rain,
When life hands you lemons, just ride on the train.
For every confusion, there's humor to find,
And laughter is solace, the best kind to bind.

Stumbling Upon Clarity in Chaos

In a world paved with puzzles, I trip on my shoes,
Chasing rabbits in circles, oh, what do I choose?
With breadcrumbs for guidance, a curious trail,
I tumble and giggle, in absurd fairy tale.

The more I seek answers, the fuzzier they get,
Like socks in a dryer, all tangled and wet.
But in my missteps, a glimpse of the light,
I laugh at the nonsense, it feels just right.

A banana in pajamas is leading my path,
With monkeys reciting the whole aftermath.
If chaos is comfort, then I'm truly blessed,
Stumbling through nonsense, I'm always impressed.

So here's to the mishaps, the trips and the falls,
To dancing in circles and bouncing off walls.
In chaos's embrace, I find my true state,
Where clarity tickles, and laughter is fate.

www.ingramcontent.com/pod-product-compliance
Lightning Source LLC
Chambersburg PA
CBHW051651160426
43209CB00004B/878